Spiritual Classics
Series

World Wisdom
The Library of Perennial Philosophy

The Library of Perennial Philosophy is dedicated to the exposition of the timeless Truth underlying the diverse religions. This Truth, often referred to as the *Sophia Perennis*—or Perennial Wisdom—finds its expression in the revealed Scriptures as well as the writings of the great sages and the artistic creations of the traditional worlds.

The Quiet Way appears as one of our selections in the Spiritual Classics series.

Spiritual Classics Series

This series includes seminal, but often neglected, works of unique spiritual insight from leading religious authors of both the East and West. Ranging from books composed in ancient India to forgotten jewels of our time, these important classics feature new introductions which place them in the perennialist context.

Reader. God is your beginning; if you have Him in essence,
You have already read the conclusion of this book. . .

                                   Gerhard Tersteegen

The Quiet Way

A Christian Path to Inner Peace

⤙⤜

Gerhard Tersteegen

Translated by
Emily Chisholm

Introduction by
Peter C. Erb

World Wisdom

The Quiet Way:
A Christian Path to Inner Peace
Gerhard Tersteegen

©2008 World Wisdom, Inc.

Library of Congress Cataloging-in-Publication Data

Tersteegen, Gerhard, 1697-1769.
  [Correspondence. English Selections.]
  The quiet way : a Christian path to inner peace / Gerhard Tersteegen ;
translated by Emily Chisholm ; introduction by Peter C. Erb.
      p. cm. – (Spiritual classics series) (The library of perennial philoso-
phy)
  Includes bibliographical references and index.
  ISBN 978-1-933316-52-9 (pbk. : alk. paper) 1. Mysticism–Early works
to 1800. I. Chisholm, Emily. II. Title.
  BV5082.3.T47 2008
  248.2'2–dc22

                                                        2007050290

Printed on acid-free paper in Canada

For information address World Wisdom, Inc.
P.O. Box 2682, Bloomington, Indiana 47402-2682

www.worldwisdom.com

Contents

Translator's Preface

These extracts from letters are translated from German written two hundred-and-fifty years ago, but scarcely a phrase of them has dated. Indeed, they might have been composed expressly to meet our problems today.

Germany, at the beginning of the eighteenth century, was war-ridden and morally and spiritually impoverished. A thirty-years' war had cost her twelve million lives, four-fifths of her population, and had left behind it a land of ravaged farmsteads, destroyed stock, famine, disease, bestiality and even cannibalism.

Religion was at its lowest ebb. In 1686 there was not a single copy of the Bible or New Testament in any bookshop in Leipzig. Yet in this darkness there glowed a few embers of the pure fire which were in time to enlighten Germany, and, by warming the heart of John Wesley, revive religion in England.

These tiny flames were held by a few men, who preached that religion was not an affair of the brain, not the involved doctrines spun by learned theologians, but, first and foremost, the heart and will devoted in love to God and one's neighbor. God, they said, was no respecter of persons. He would use the simplest soul who believed and loved as His priest.

To Gerhard Tersteegen, an apprentice shop-keeper in Mülheim, "a godly merchant" came as God's priest and led his soul into peace. But the constant bustle of shopkeeping proved too much for his delicate health, and he retired to the more peaceful work of ribbon-weaving. In an isolated cottage Tersteegen lived alone with his God and his books, helped only by a little girl who came once a day to wind his silk.

For five years Gerhard was "deprived of the sense of God's favor" till one day, when he was walking along a country road, "the Dayspring from on high visited him." He signed a covenant with God in his blood and the cottage became a center of spiritual power. Tersteegen's reputation as a good man and a spiritual adviser spread through the neighborhood and to the four corners of Germany. He had a vast correspondence with numerous "brothers and sisters" who wrote for his spiritual counsel, and there were usually twenty to thirty people in his waiting-room every evening. When he preached, the cottage was crammed with some four to five hundred people, often including strangers from Holland, Switzerland, or England. So great was the desire to hear him speak that ladders were fetched from the farms, set up at the open windows, and people listened, perched on the rungs. Even the king, Frederick the Great, heard of the wisdom of the saintly weaver and summoned him to the palace at Wesel for conversations.

Tersteegen's advice was simple. You are the child of God. God's nature is in you. It has only become overclouded. Withdraw from outward things. Pray, and you will make contact again with God, the source of your being. Forget yourself. Forget your selfish desires. Look to God. Die to your own will, live for God's will and you will know true life.

The following extracts are Tersteegen's advice to people harassed by war-time conditions, uncongenial companions, religious doubts, bad tempers, church divisions, uncontrollable impulses, and the will to do good which seems so often to be overruled by the bent to do evil.

For all of these Tersteegen has answers warm with charity and deep spiritual insight, as applicable now as on the day they were first penned.

Emily Chisholm

Historical Introduction

Born in Moers on the Lower Rhine in 1697, Gerhard Tersteegen grew up in a diverse religious area, including all three major Christian confessions: Reformed, Lutheran, and Roman Catholic. Among the Protestant Reformed and Lutheran traditions he experienced further division, particularly in the early part of his life, by the ongoing controversy between the Orthodox factions and those who were designated Pietists. Before his death in 1769 at Mülheim on the Ruhr, Christians as a whole and he with them would be facing the impact of the Enlightenment and the onslaught of secular modernity.

Tersteegen struggled with all these complexities from within a wing of the Pietist tradition, often referred to as Radical Pietism.[1] Raised within a Reformed

---

[1] For a general overview of this movement see Carter Lindberg

(Calvinist) framework, Tersteegen lost his father, a textile merchant, at an early age, but was able nevertheless to gain a good humanistic education and a command of Latin, Greek, Hebrew, French, and Dutch as well as some Spanish along with his native German. Too poor to attend university, in 1712 he was apprenticed to his uncle, a merchant at Mülheim on the Ruhr, where, in the midst of a spiritual crisis in his late teens he encountered pietistic groups, all of whom owed much to the earlier activity of the Reformed pastor Theodor Undereyck in the town, and the ongoing influence of the "founder" of the Pietist movement, Philip Jakob

(ed.), *The Pietist Theologians* (Oxford, 2005; the collection includes an essay on Tersteegen by Hansgünter Ludewig, 190-206) and my *Pietists* (New York, 1983). For a full discussion of such figures see Martin Brecht, *Geschichte des Pietismus*, 2 vols. (Göttingen, 1993, 1995) and in particular the sections by Hans Schneider, "Der radikale Pietismus im 17. Jahrhundert," 1:391-437, and "Der radikale Pietismus im 18. Jahrhundert," 2: 107-97.

Spener (1635-1705), the former superintendent of the Lutheran ministerium in Frankfurt am Main.

In 1675 Spener had published an introduction to the sermons of Johann Arndt (1555-1621),[2] later printed separately under the title *Pia Desideria: Or, Heartfelt Desires for a God-pleasing Improvement of the True Protestant Church.*[3] The *Pia Desideria* outlined Spener's hopes and intentions under five headings. After noting the decline in moral life at the time, it detailed at length the defects of political and clerical authorities as well as those of the populace, clarified the possibility of reform, and set down proposals to enact it. Scripture

[2] For details see my edition and translation of Johann Arndt, *True Christianity* (New York, 1979).

[3] *Pia desideria: Oder hertzliches Verlangen, nach Gottefälliger Besserung der wahren Evangelischen Kirchen, sampt einigen dahin einfaltig abzweckenden Christlichen Vorschlägen . . . Sampt angehengten zweyer Christlichen Theologorum darüber gestellten, und zu mehrer aufferbauung höchst-dienlichen Bedencken* (Franckfurt am Mayn, 1676).

reading by individuals was emphasized and a call made for sermons which would treat the biblical text in context. It was at this point in the argument that Spener outlined his proposal for the use of group meetings to stimulate Christian growth. Discussion of such conventicles led Spener to his second proposal: the necessity of practicing the spiritual priesthood of all believers. A call for the practice of piety was the *Pia Desideria*'s third proposal, and the specific characteristic of this piety was developed in the final proposals, pressing Christians to come to agreement through dedicated prayer, examples of moral well-being, and heartfelt love. The mark of the true Christian was above all signalled by experience, evidenced in a genuine sense of one's own sinfulness and heartfelt repentance (*Busse*), the New Birth in Christ (*Wiedergeburt*), and an ongoing Christian devotion and work centered on the love of God and neighbor.

Such principles seemed to many of Spener's contemporaries to be based on a questionable theology, which relegated doctrine to a secondary position and elevated experiential piety, personal assurance, and a high moral and devotional life, in practice if not in theory, to the rank of saving graces—a return to the "works' righteousness," "theology of human glory" religion so firmly rejected by Luther and his doctrine of forensic justification "by faith alone."

Despite this, Pietist concerns spread rapidly and by Tersteegen's youth had affected Protestant denominations in Germany, Holland, and Switzerland, and were carried to the Germanic-speaking areas of North America. Many of the adherents of the movement remained within the organized churches of their birth and saw in the Pietist spirit, the form and power by which their various congregations and traditions might be revitalized. Many others, however, the radical

Pietists, moved in the direction towards which Spener's enemies saw the whole revival oriented. Some of these, in fact, separated themselves from the churches with which they had initially been associated, forming new sectarian bodies as they did. It was within this latter framework that the work and life of Tersteegen was fixed.

In the midst of his religious search Tersteegen was fortunate in gaining the friendship of a spiritual director, Wilhelm Hoffmann (1685-1746), a follower of the separatist and mystically-oriented radical Ernst Christian Hochmann v. Hochenau (1670-1721) and a committed reader of sixteenth and seventeenth century Roman Catholic mystics (particularly Madame Guyon [1647-1717] and the Quietists of the time) as well as their medieval precursors.[4] Following his con-

---

[4] On the use of mystical texts among these radicals see my *Pietists,*

version after Pentecost, 1717, Tersteegen gave up his trade, supporting himself thereafter as a weaver so as to enter into the fullest contemplation, following the life of Jesus, initially experiencing visions and "dark nights of the soul," questioning the existence of God in the face of so many diverse and opposing religious options. A "breakthrough" was granted him however and he gained an assurance of God's existence, knowing in a "moment" the essential enlightening presence of the Lord in the ground of the soul, "the inner experiential knowledge that brings with it the power making one holy, and the embracing love of the divine."

With the discovery of this divine spark in the self, one discovered one's true self, Tersteegen taught—a self open to growth as the "I" (ego) of self-will and self-seeking was given up, as one gave oneself over in

Protestants, and Mysticism: The Use of Late Medieval Spiritual Texts in the Work of Gottfried Arnold (1666-1714) (Metuchen, N.J., 1989).

Gelassenheit (resignation) to God. His thought owes much to the work of the early patristic writer Macarius whom he knew through the edition of Gottfried Arnold (1666-1714)[5] and his own reading of Jean Bernières de Louvigny's (1602-1659) *The Hidden Life of Christ in God*,[6] a work widely circulated in Tersteegen's translation. Tersteegen nevertheless remains fully a Protestant in his emphasis on the grace, received by faith alone, that first grants the enlightenment in Christ. The point

[5] Details in *Pietists, Protestants, and Mysticism.* For an English translation see *Pseudo Macarius, The Fifty Spiritual Homilies and the Great Letter,* translated, edited, with an introduction by George A. Maloney (New York, 1992).

[6] *Das verborgene Leben mit Christo in Gott. Auf eine recht-Evangelische Weise entdecket, und nach seinen wesentlichen Eigenschafften und Wirckungen, vormals in Französis. Sprache beschrieben von . . . Johann von Bernières Louvignii. Anjetzo, aus allen dessen gottseligen Schrifften, in teutscher Sprache kürtzlich zusammen gezogen, und in dreyen Büchlein abgefasset . . . samt einer Vorrede des Ausgebers* (Franckfurt & Leipzig, 1728).

is explicitly made in his 1724 Maundy Thursday letter, written in his own blood to Jesus, his savior and redeemer. By this indwelling of the hidden life with Christ in and before God one can grow, always in and by grace, toward the fulfillment of one's salvation in Christ. This theology had an ecumenical orientation, but one in keeping with and intensifying Protestant teaching. It regarded the invisible church to which all true believers, including Roman Catholics, belonged, as the only way to consider Christian unity. More firmly than his fellow Pietists, Tersteegen tended to denigrate the institutional forms of the established churches, even of his Protestant co-believers and, as a result, misread the sacramental "objectivity" and commitment to the visible Church on the part of the Catholic mystics he admired.

Following his "second conversion" in 1724, Tersteegen began to offer instruction in his home, writing hymns and publishing his highly popular collection the *Geistliches Blumengärtlein inniger Seelen*[7] ("Spiritual Flower-garden of Interior Souls") in 1729, translating mystical writing (note particularly his *Auserlesenen Lebensbeschreibungen Heiliger Seelen*[8] ["Selected Biographies of Holy Souls" 1733-1753]), and composing his own works in the evening hours following his necessary work (he gave up the latter in 1728 for health reasons), speaking publicly when requested and offering extensive spiritual direction not only to the "monastic" community of the "Pilgerhütte" that developed around him, but to the many circles of his adherents in neighboring and more distant areas. In the late 1730s the

---

[7] *Geistliches Blumen-Gärtlein inniger Seelen; oder kurtze Schluss-Reimen, Betrachtungen und Lieder über allerhand Warheiten des inwendigen Christenthums* . . . Dritte und vermehrte Edition. Nebst *der Frommen Lotterie* (Franckfurt & Leipzig, 1738).

[8] *Auserlesene Lebensbeschreibungen heiliger Seelen: in welchen nebst derselben merkwürdigen aussern Lebens-Historie* Dritte Edition (3 Bde.; Essen: Zacharias Bädeker, 1784).

Tersteegen movement suffered some persecution and he took a more reserved approach to his public appearances, but by the mid-1740s he once again spoke openly as the result of a revival in the area under the Dutch student of theology, Jacob Chevalier. In 1746 he had moved to a house beside the Church of St. Peter, where he often preached to large groups until 1756, despite continuing opposition from local religious authorities.

His influence continued to grow even after his death and extended into the mainline churches, in Germany especially during the great awakening of the early nineteenth century (*Erweckungsbewegung*) and in the English-speaking churches particularly through his hymns, translated into English by John Wesley (1703-1791) in the eighteenth century[9] and in the following

[9] See Paul Wagner, *John Wesley and the German Pietist Heritage: The*

century by Catherine Winkworth (1827-1878).[10]

His productivity can be measured to some extent by considering his published works. He wrote over one hundred hymns and some 1500 verse fragments, and the number of his sermons and spiritual letters have been estimated at 15,000, filling over 5000 printed pages, of which the mere 100 in Emily Chisholm's translation that follow offer a tantalizing and selective, but representative, taste for the whole. They serve as a companion volume for her *Gerhard Tersteegen: Sermons and Hymns* (Shoals, n.d.,), but aside from these works

Development of Hymnody, PhD diss. (Toronto School of Theology, University of Toronto, 2004), and compare John L. Nuelsen, *John Wesley und das Deutsche Kierchenlied* (Nashville, Tenn., 1938), translated by Theo Parry, Sidney H. Moore, and Arthur Holbrook, *John Wesley and the German Hymn* (Yorkshire, 1972).

[10] *Lyra Germanica, First Series: Songs of the Household* (London: G. Routledge, 1855) and *Lyra Germanica, Second Series: The Christian Life* (London: Longman, Green, Longman, and Roberts, 1858).

relatively little of his writing has been translated for the English reader,[11] making these words all the more precious.

Considering the paucity of translations, one may admire Wesley in particular for his decision to translate Tersteegen's "Verborgene Gottes Liebe, Du"[12] (forgiving the freedom he at times takes with the original text and the reduction of ten stanzas to eight), a hymn that sums up as it were Tersteegen's spirituality and provides thus the best introduction to his letters:

> Thou hidden love of God, whose height,
> Whose depth unfathomed, no man knows,
> I see from far thy beauteous light,

---

[11] Note *Constraining Love: and other Selections from the Writings of Gerhard Tersteegen*, edited by H.E. Govan (Edinburgh, 1928).

[12] *Geistliches Blumen-Gärtlein inniger Seelen*, 3:26.

Inly I sigh for thy repose;
My heart is pained, nor can it be
At rest, till it finds rest in thee.

Thy secret voice invites me still
The sweetness of thy yoke to prove;
And fain I would; but though my will
Seems fixed, yet wide my passions rove;
Yet hindrances strew all the way;
I aim at thee, yet from thee stray.

'Tis mercy all, that thou hast brought
My mind to seek her peace in thee;
Yet, while I seek but find thee not,
No peace my wandering soul shall see;
O when shall all my wanderings end,
And all my steps to thee-ward tend!

Is there a thing beneath the sun
That strives with thee my heart to share?

Ah, tear it thence, and reign alone,
The Lord of every motion there!
Then shall my heart from earth be free,
When it hath found repose in thee.

O hide this self from me, that I
No more, but Christ in me, may live!
My vile affections crucify,
Nor let one darling lust survive
In all things nothing may I see,
Nothing desire or seek, but thee!

O Love, thy sovereign aid impart,
To save me from low-thoughted care;
Chase this self-will through all my heart,
Through all its latent mazes there,
Make me thy duteous child, that I
Ceaseless may, "Abba, Father," cry!

Ah no! ne'er will I backward turn;
Thine wholly, thine alone, I am:
Thrice happy he who views with scorn
Earth's toys, for thee his constant flame!
O help, that I may never move
From the blest footsteps of thy love!

Each moment draw from earth away
My heart, that lowly waits thy call;
Speak to my inmost soul, and say,
"I am thy love, thy God, thy all!"
To feel thy power, to hear thy voice,
To taste thy love, be all my choice.

Fittingly, Tersteegen himself opens the volume from
which Wesley selected this hymn in an address "to the
Reader":

*Mensch, Gott dein Anfang ist; hast du ihn
   selbst im Wesen,*
*So hast du schon das End von dieser
   Schrift gelesen. . .*

Reader. God is your beginning; if you have
   him in essence,
You have already read the conclusion of
   this book. . .

Peter C. Erb
Wilfrid Laurier University, Canada

The Blessed Journey

Is. xlii. 16.

Let Him lead thee blindfold onwards,
Love needs not to know;
Children whom the Father leadeth
Ask not where they go.
Though the path be all unknown,
Over moors and mountains lone.

Give no ear to reason's questions:
Let the blind man hold
That the sun is but a fable
Men believed of old.
At the breast the babe will grow;
Whence the milk he need not know.

1

God, Our True Life

We are conscious these days of a deep-seated hunger, a secret need in our heart's core, to be set free from sin, from the world, and from self-centeredness, and so to be reunited with our source. We must only be in earnest about it. The power is close at hand.

Just stay where you are and unite yourselves with God as with something there already, that you do not need to seek! For God is certainly with you and in you, although hidden by darkness.

It is true that this Something to which your heart inclines is not known by you clearly; but this not-knowing is true knowing, and this undefined, better than a thousand definitions.

You don't need to search for God; you have only to realize Him.

The mind of God and the light of God do not come in from outside. They do not borrow their certainty and strength from our minds or our senses. They make themselves known in the heart's core and have both energy and certainty in themselves, although these become darkened and disappear when the soul begins to search after clear certainty in her depths. So do not go out so much into reflections. Do not seek merely by reasoned, external methods to find sure foundations, but close your eyes like a child and confide yourself to the hidden Being who is so near to you inwardly.

O that I could pour out my whole heart in tears and weep for the blindness of men! They take their deceptive illusions and their trivial things for the essential, and the essential things of the spirit for imagination and error. Yet it has been told us aforctime that the natural man, in contrast to the spiritual, can perceive nothing of the things of the Spirit of God.

What is visible is passing; the best in it comes and goes.

We see, we admire, we bury ourselves in things which are not, and Him who is, we leave out of consideration.

All we children of Adam live in time; and we can neither comprehend nor criticize the eternal and infinite with our finite reason. We see God in parts, so to speak, now from this side, now from that, and what we cannot make into rhyme or reason, we try to isolate, and will not believe to be God. Then we fashion God after our own idea and draw our own consequences and conclusions; and anything which does not agree with them, we must, of course, contradict. And it is just in this way, in my opinion, that many ugly theories and errors have arisen among all sections of Christendom.

Oh, what a difference when, after reason has carved an image of God, the Lord himself comes and impresses His glorious knowledge and His very self upon the soul!

I esteem no books to be more superfluous in the world than those which set out to prove that there is a God. Since so many millions of people have been in America, no books are needed to prove that there is a New World.

The witness of grace in the heart and conscience is the best guarantee of truth, and anyone who keeps to this will never be led astray by any error. To self-activated reason this is a piece of foolishness.

Where *we* stop doing and worrying, God begins, and He will be everything in our nothingness.

God is all-sufficient in every way. He is able, He alone is able. He is perfectly able. He is able to satisfy and bless the incredibly great receptivity of our soul.

May the Lord grant us living experience of this Being in our souls, even although we should at the same time forget all we know about it.

It is a little thing for Him to let us find in our souls in one moment, without any trouble, what we may have been seeking for years with such trouble outside ourselves.

In general you must overcome all evil, all distractions, yes, and the whole world, not by force and restlessness, but by calm suffering and contempt, by forgetting and closing your eyes. There is Another in us who is fighting for us. Look to Him lovingly.

There are still many good souls today, but few true worshipers of God's will. We live too much in ourselves and our good intentions.

Our dear brother writes that he has so many cruel adversaries who have left him stripped even of the shadow of outward honor, but that is a good start, a palisade fencing him in and keeping him from sallying forth. Let all that is personal to us rot away! Let the whole world die for us and all creatures abandon us; we would only become free, more fitted to hear the Lord, follow the Lord, and enjoy Him in the blessed wilderness of inner solitude. Oh, that our whole being might remain turned toward Him alone! When we enjoy esteem from others or have anything else, knowledge, or ability in the physical or the spiritual realm, it is so incredibly easy to bring some of the plunder with us to our intercourse with God, but that is not lawful merchandise. We should come naked, give ourselves blindly and entirely to love, and, empty of will, empty of activity, leave ourselves in the hands of love that He may fashion us, order us and use us at His good pleasure for His purposes. The longer we practice this discipline, the more we experience of the blessed mercilessness of God's love: how He brings to nought, destroys and rejects all that is not His own work, how He draws everything to Himself and absorbs it, that at last He may live and work in us and through us and reign alone as king. Happy the soul who refuses nothing to love, but places everything at His disposal: for only thus may all our works be done more and more in God.

What we ourselves do is truly of no use whatever. The less we ourselves are in our doing, the purer and more useful it is.

To obey is better than sacrifice. We must serve God in His way, not ours.

In short, I realize more and more that what I do is unavailing, but everything avails when I let God do it.

And yet it is really not necessary for you to know much about yourself and your state. It would be better for you and me to be quite unconscious of ourselves.

Let us forget ourselves.

Your sensuous nature is mercurial, sensitive, touchy: if it finds no nourishment in creatures and creature comforts, it seeks it in the spiritual realm, desiring to clutch God and all God's good gifts to itself. Well, as the Lord, for your good, is not allowing much to flow in to your sensuous nature (you can feel no sweet consolations), your nature takes on a disgruntled, irritable temper and like a dog who has no bone, is biting at a stone.

And, since self-love lies at the bottom of it, spiritual poverty is the end of it. What is to be done? Just follow God in His healing guidance which aims at destroying your self-love and making you capable of loving Him with a direct outflowing of all your heart, just as self-love is a crooked turning into ourselves. He has put something into your heart, which yearns to be entirely and eternally God's; this inclination lies there, deep, dark, and all-embracing.

You must withdraw into yourself a little and keep quiet before the face of God, then look gently and perfectly frankly at God who is so near to us, to let Him see if there is anything in us or near us which must be handed over, and assure Him of our hearty consent to give up everything to Him. Remain exposed to Him in the light of truth simply, in this way, without any investigations or scruples of your own, for as long as God gives grace.

Since then, I am neither willing nor able to row against the wind, I let my little ship go in it. If only I take care not to stick fast on some sandbank of selfishness, let come what may, even if I suffer shipwreck, it will only be in the ocean of God, whose depths are as good as the best harbor.

I do not as yet desire the death of the body, but that death I do desire where I can neither find nor see myself anymore.

The Opened Eyes

John ix. 37.

"Where is a God?" doth weary Reason say—
"I see but starlit skies."
"Where is the sun?" So calleth at noonday
The man with sightless eyes.
Thou, little child, from thee God is not far;
Look inwards, not above:
Thou needest not to roam from star to star,
For God is Love.

2

The Closer Walk

The loadstone of His love has touched and magnetized the iron (I mean the needle of our spirit); its desire and its whole tendency is toward Him and Him alone: but oh! how restless, how trembling the poor needle becomes when a strange power or some intermediary stops it, or seems to stop it, from going where it will. Let be; it longs to go there, longs intensely. He who draws it to himself, knows that it looks to Him and Him alone, and His power of attraction is enough to bring all opposition to nought, so that at last the spirit may yield itself freely and be inwardly at one with Him.

Give yourselves over to God and to His unhindered will for time and eternity. Drop all anxiety for yourselves, so that you would no longer want to look to yourselves, even if you knew that you were on the road to hell. What do yourselves matter? What does the self matter? Just think. Suppose your wretched state became still worse and continued till death and you were damned for eternity; accept it all and say: "Nevertheless I will not sin, nevertheless I will still love and glorify God. What do I matter?" Dispose yourself in this way in every situation in which the soul may find herself. In this way surrender leads into pure love and your bitter, restless motions will pass into a deep and gentle peace, and your oppression into an immeasurable breadth and freedom of the spirit.

The inner will must not keep swaying in the balance but swing right over to the side of God. Then

God will give it invincible strength. Oh, if only we came close to our God in faith and love, whole mountains of hindrances, miseries, and weaknesses would disappear like a mere straw in a great fire.

If He only has the heart, the thoughts will follow it in the end.

All good intentions, impulses, desires, or thoughts are not our own productions, but God's working in us, which we must neither suppress nor avoid, but accept and remain in it. We must not think as if God worked good in us only at one particular time and then went away, leaving us in the lurch to carry on by ourselves. By no means! At the very moment when we find a good intention, desire, or impulse in ourselves and for as long as we find it in ourselves, there is the Lord our God, inwardly near, making it and keeping it, the true source of all good within us. He creates in us the will to good, and desires most heartily to bring the good in us to fruition—but, in accordance with His good pleasure,[1] not our own ideas. We should simply remain in God in all fidelity, giving full scope to His working in us and continually expecting new powers, while we remain in Him, the source. Yes, even when we experience our own weakness and disloyalty, instead of losing heart, we should turn inwards once again, and with bowed head, seek the strength for renewal at the right place.

A man must first *find* his soul before he can *lose* it, otherwise his loss is only a fancied loss and really does him harm. This loss or abandonment of the self in God is a pure and noble work of God, which, at the cost of distress and death to one's own life, transplants

[1] Philippians 2:13.

the soul into God. When I hear anyone talk cheerfully and even jocularly about this, I think I have reason to believe that such a one has not yet had the experience. Only very few souls really attain to it, for the majority require a very different diet. In some cases, self-love seizes hold of the ideal, regarding it as a prize: but this kind of loss and surrender only produces a fluttering, frivolous character. Such souls talk about loss, but obviously they still hold fast and live completely in themselves. Now because I know that the soul is never transferred to God and His life, except by God Himself and His working within, and that God cannot work freely when we do not worship Him by suffering and keeping a quiet mind, I recommend to everyone contemplation and prayer, according to his ability, whether he works or suffers.

The Name Above Every Name

Luke i. 31.

Name of Jesus! highest Name!
Name that earth and Heaven adore!
From the heart of God it came,
Leads me to God's heart once more.

Name of Jesus! living tide!
Days of drought for me are past;
How much more than satisfied,
Are the thirsty lips at last!

Name of Jesus! dearest Name!
Bread of Heaven, and balm of love,
Oil of gladness, surest claim
To the treasures stored above.

Jesus gives forgiveness free,
Jesus cleanses all my stains,
Jesus gives His life to me,
Jesus always He remains.

Only Jesus! fairest Name!
Life, and rest, and peace, and bliss;
Jesus, evermore the same,
He is mine, and I am His.

3

Prayer

In God's eyes, everything done for love of Him is prayer.

Pray, if you like, without words, but never without worship.

Perhaps you do not yet give yourself wholeheartedly enough to the Lord; perhaps you only give yourself superficially, and not entirely and in everything; perhaps you only give yourself in so far as you would like to guard yourself from sin and live blamelessly in outward things—which is certainly good, but not enough. You must give Him your whole will, your whole heart, your dearest and your best.

Perhaps you do it too hastily and abruptly. One must stand still for a little, worshiping with the heart; it must be deliberate and from the heart, even when one has to suffer many undesired distractions.

What is easier and simpler than to open one's eyes and see the light which surrounds us on all sides? God is far closer to us than the light. In Him we live and move and have our being. He comes into us, He fills us; He is nearer than we are to ourselves; to believe this simply and to remember this simply, as well as one can, is prayer.

Time for prayer one can and must purchase dearly; proficiency in it, we can neither buy nor give ourselves. We must come as we are, so that God may make us as we should be.

You say you cannot pray. Is there then no *Oh* and no *Ah* in your heart? And, granted you cannot find even that, when you say you cannot pray, you are praying.

In meditation, love and sincerity must hold the rudder. All thoughts and fancies which keep intruding in spite of the will, can then be endured—from which endurance sheer salvation is born.

When you have surrendered yourself to God of a morning and made a good resolve, you must not imagine, worship over, you will now set about your household affairs and turn to outward things. O, it is no wonder, then, that you are estranged from God and drawn into all sorts of distractions. If our resolve is to be constant, we will have to learn humbly to remain with God and in God and try to hold the devotion we have felt; for in God is our strength.

Let deep call unto deep! And let this be your prayer when you cannot make any other.

Prayer is looking at God, who is ever present, and letting Him look on us.

We do not need to bring this thing or that, put ourselves into this or that attitude, or see or feel much every time we pray. We must just say simply and briefly what we are and what we would like to be; yes, it is not even necessary always to *say* it, we should just allow God, the ever-present, all-loving one to see us thus—but not perfunctorily: we should try to keep close in front of Him for some time, that He may have a good look at us and cure us. We must tell Him nothing and let Him see nothing but what is in us, whatever it may be.

Well, when you find yourself distracted, gloomy, or insensitive, tell God simply and let Him see your misery: that is true prayer.

The God of love who is close to us, touches our spirit with His love and draws us to Himself. And so our spirit becomes so moved by impulses and inclinations that it can find rest henceforth in no other thing than God. When any soul remains in this state by dint of meditation, clears out of the way by self-denial all that might hinder the spirit in its progress, and by complete surrender into the hands of God follows this its root-inclination, lo, this root-inclination becomes a kind of gravitation of love, leading the spirit to God, just as a little brook flows down to the ocean, and just as a stone thrown into the air, sinks down on to the earth which is its center.

This, then, is the practice of *inward prayer*—to remain close to this root-inclination.

But, I understand by prayer, not so much the asking, demanding and beseeching of the soul to obtain this or that from God, but every activity of our spirit and our faith with God and the things of God; and, in general, what is called in Scripture, a walk with God.

If you have particular things to pray for, give them a childlike glance which says it all at the beginning of the prayer; then forget all about it and merge yourself into the universal need of men, wherein, without thinking of individual requirements, you ask everything for everybody.

Oil and Wine

Is. xxxv. 10.

There is a balm for every pain,
A medicine for all sorrow;
The eye turned backward to the Cross,
And forward to the morrow.
The morrow of the glory and the psalm,
When He shall come;
The morrow of the harping and the palm,
The welcome home.
Meantime in His beloved hands our ways,
And on His Heart the wandering heart at rest;
And comfort for the weary one who lays
His head upon His Breast.

4

Comfort in Sorrow

The storm and tempest of the sufferings of our time rush past us like a short, troubled dream: and then we will rest in God for ever.

Think and care in no wise about what is to come. Love and suffer in the present moment, thinking more about God and His strength than of yourself and your weakness. If increase of suffering comes, increase of grace will come also.

Do not think ahead and do not look back! Both bring unrest and are harmful to you in your present condition. The present moment must be your dwelling-place. There only can we find God and His will.

When Christ rose with His disciples from the supper of love and communion, He went with them into the garden of Gethsemane. He still walks with us in this way. Willing consent to suffering and death is the first and best fruit of a true communion with God. Rising from this table of intercourse with God by faith, the soul must be able to say with the Redeemer: "That the world may know that I love the Father.... Arise, let us go hence."[2]

Drink then to the very dregs the cup handed to you by no enemy and no stranger, but by your Father.

This, however, is certain. God never deprives us of something, be it temporal or spiritual, except to impart Himself in His very essence, after we have had the necessary preparation.

[2] John 14:31.

You ask whether I only love and praise? Or whether I am still suffering as well? I do all three at the same time, nor would I ask to do any of these by itself on earth. Suffering without love is for the damned; love without suffering is for the blessed. Here on earth we honor God by both as the children of love, crucified.

Not, "Come down from the cross" but, with head bowed, in blind submission, say with Christ: "Father, into Thy hands I commit my spirit."

Say little or nothing to others about your suffering. Enough for you that the Lord, your God, sees it.

It is not in pleasantness and enjoyment that we know ourselves. The cross must reveal what we are.

To be a burden to oneself, and yet to be obliged to carry oneself, is valiant suffering.

It is with us as with Peter: when we look at Jesus, we are brave and we can walk over the waves; but if we look at ourselves and the waves, we sink.[3]

The Lord gives a cross according to strength—or strength according to the cross.

A time of suffering and adversity is our harvest-tide, when we endure rain and travail for the sake of that magnificent fruit, obedience.

May the Lord grant us this, that although our body be crucified and our soul darkened, our spirit may still remain joyful and quiet in our God.

Faith, in its essence and its root, is the springing of new life given by the grace of God. See, this is our work, praying.

[3] Matthew 14:30.

I would rather a thousand times that you were ill near God, than well far from Him.

Perhaps He has wanted to take you specially aside by means of this illness, because he has some message of love to give you. Speak peace then, O Lord, for Thy handmaiden heareth! For certainly God's presence and inward comfort can make a sickbed a Paradise.

Bear your cross with love, and if you have to bear yourself at the same time, let it be with peaceful humility.

Childhood

Is. xxxii. 3.

Soul, journeying through the desert wild,
Could thou become a little child,
Thou wouldst behold with joyful eyes
God walking in His Paradise.

A little child, submissive, still,
That knoweth not it hath a will—
What mother gives, it simply takes,
And sweetly sleeps, and laughing wakes.

If taken up, or laid at rest,
All comes to it as it were best;
If all forget it for a while,
It has no language but a smile.

To it alike are praise or blame,
Alike a king's or peasant's name—
A thing so weak, so poor, so small,
Yet fearing nought that may befall.

How true and innocent its eyes!
And simply trusting, it is wise.
It reasons not, nor looks before,
The present moment all its store.

It cannot walk, nor stand alone,
And nothing doth it call its own—
It knows no dangers, no alarms,
Safe sheltered in its mother's arms.

Of learnèd lore, and tangled thought,
And questions deep, it knoweth nought,
And void of wonder or surprise,
It watches all with sunny eyes.

It has its little joy and bliss,
Its mother's arms, its mother's kiss—
Her face is ever its delight,
Its comfort sweet by day and night.

Blest innocence of childish days!
So unto me are Wisdom's ways;
A love divinely deep and high—
Oh would that such a child were I!

The life of God in me begun,
Filled with the Spirit of His Son,
In childhood of the life divine,
Untroubled trust and gladness mine.

Whilst yet through desert wilds I roam,
A child in the eternal Home;
Beholding now, with joyful eyes,
God walking in His Paradise.

5

As Little Children

There are many ways, means, and preparations, whereby we may gain reunion and fellowship with God. But the nearest way of all, and the easiest means, yes, the tiny point where this union is actually achieved, is when we become little children. The Son of God became one with mankind as a child, and mankind can only be united to God in the state of spiritual childhood. And, indeed, dear sister, the baby Jesus constrains us once again to enter with Him into the most perfect innocence of the childlike mind. So, away with all scruples, brooding, suspicion, unrest, and all lovelessness.

When I spoke to him for a short time, I did notice that he was not willing just then to sink right down into simplicity, but I thought that it would come of itself when we knew one another better; for, beside his uncommon cleverness, knowledge, and talents, I perceived that he certainly had a feeling for God. I loved him for it and love him still. But with such people, who have eaten so much of the tree of knowledge, one must have great patience. The way is hard enough for us and others too, before we become really simple and willing to take upon ourselves, undaunted, the shame of Christ; how much more difficult it is for such as he? Let us just be onlookers for a while! By cross and distress God can still bring many a one down from the seat of the scorner, so that later he will gladly sit down among the children.

Through prayer the poorest and most wicked child of man can become a holy child of God, even if you do not see and feel it at once and all the time. The child often drinks his mother's milk without realizing it, or in sleep, and is being fed unawares.

To be a child is your calling. Listen to no other gospel: in it alone you will find rest.

Do not make so many conjectures about the future. How will things turn out in the end? Will you ever be saved? And so on. These are the fruits and thoughts of reason, not of faith. Does a baby make himself ill with worrying if he will ever become a perfect full-grown man? He just sucks, eats, and drinks with a good courage and grows imperceptibly, for time soon shows whether he will grow and how big he will be. So do you also. Trust the Lord to do His work, and walk with Him as with a beloved bosom-friend, in all simplicity and sincerity of heart.

We should be like children with one another and, as such, behave in all simplicity. In this way we will make fewest mistakes. The truly childlike intention of walking in God's ways will not look at the contrary notions of reason, but let them vanish in the presence of the Lord, without stopping to give them a glance.

A child is weak, careless and often breaks or spoils something. The father punishes or disciplines the child, but he will not chase him out of the house for it; he is still his child, deeply moved because he has hurt his father and promising to do better. This promise is childish enough, but it is childlike and, what is more, it comes front the heart. The father sees it and is pleased, although he knows the child's weakness very well.

And see, dear brother, it is the same with our acts, our undertakings, and our promises, which we must rate neither too high nor too low. We place them *too high* when we treat a serious intention as the achievement itself, or as if we were able to keep to it, and carry it out as planned.

We place them *too low* when we consider them as our own productions, and when we experience again and again our own disloyalty and backsliding; we let everything go and give no more time to good resolves under the apparent pretext that we would not be able to keep them.

The inability is in us; but the ability to persevere to the end is in God, and our inability is meant to drive us to Him.

Close your eyes and walk in faith and in surrender, and fear will disappear. And when the light dawns again, you will say that you have walked aright. This fear arises partly from the withdrawal of all visible strength and support. It is with you as with a little child who is always afraid of falling, while all the time his mother is holding him firmly by the reins behind, without his knowing it. But, if he stumbled or were about to fall, at once he would feel his mother's hand holding him. No, my dear child! there is no danger; your mother is near. Although she is not before your eyes. The more afraid you are, the more likely you are to stumble: but if you were about to fall, you would be conscious at once of something in you, I know not what, drawing you aside or so directing outward things that nothing would happen. Trust the hand of God, holding you, although you cannot see it, and rely on the leading-strings of His divine providence.

And, even in the greatest suffering, do you not feel within you an inextinguishable, if obscure and secret, longing for the simple, innocent, gentle, blindly trusting nature of a child and for the inner life? Yes, and from time to time, do you not feel a comforting impression coming from beyond your own understanding and outward activity, of the deep-rooted certainty that God wants you to attain it in that way.

God became a child so that the repentant might see that He forgets their sins and forgives like a child and is not angry like a hard man. This child gives us faith and confidence.

The Far and Near

Ps. lxi. 4.

In Him we live, in Him we move; seek not thy God afar;
He is not prisoned in a height above sun, moon, and star.
But thou through strange dark lands hast strayed, and wandered
far from Him;
And therfore He, O Soul, to thee, is distant and is dim.
Lord, I was in the far-off land, I loved from Thee to stray,
And when unto myself I came, a swine-herd far away,
One moment—then the welcome sweet, the kiss, the Father's Home;
Far distant was the distance; to Thy bosom I am come.

6

The Way to God

In these days, all theology, mysticism included, has been thoroughly studied by the mind; but the heart lags far behind. Not so with us, dear brother! The grace of God will not let us have any peace in appearances or a divided soul. And so be it! Let us follow the guiding of our star in a childlike spirit, however deep inwards or downwards it may lead us; for, we do already realize from afar that peace of mind and larger vision increase according as we follow this gently attracting drawing power and satisfy the demands of this inner guide, and this is irrefutable proof that our spirit is nearing the place of its peace. In the end we find the Child, and in Him, everything—peace and poverty of spirit in the solitude of Bethlehem; and the word of the prophet is fulfilled: "I will allure her, and bring her into the wilderness, and speak comfortably unto her."[4]

Blessed but secret school, where a man must give his whole will for school fees, where teaching is effective influence and learning, submission to influence, where the tiniest child sits at the top of the form and the highest wisdom is to forget everything else.

Besides, I have always believed it impossible to draw up any general system of the particular leadings of God, as one might write up the description of a journey. When enlightened souls have written about it, they have generally described *their* own particular way, for which one can glorify God, but to which one should

[4] Hosea 2:14.

not conform too rigidly. We must let the spirit of grace have a free hand in us and others.

And so I have not been very pleased to see you look out many religious books of all kinds; not in the least because I had anything against such books or such friends; but things that are good in themselves are not necessarily good for us. Many a truth, even a valuable one, may bewilder or hinder us, if we try to know it prematurely.[5]

And so my practice is to leave souls very much to the free leading of the grace of God, and to direct them only to those things to which I notice God wants to lead them, according to my reading of His will. I just watch God and caution them when they might strike something harmful. I am intimate with souls who are

[5] John 16:12.

trying sincerely and wholeheartedly to walk before God, to whom I have not said a word about books which I myself have published, because I did not consider them to be serviceable. God must be the master everywhere, and we must remain His pupils, keeping ourselves faithfully to the lesson He has set.

In answer to the rest of the letter about your distress of spirit, the following will be helpful. At the beginning, it is very useful to examine the inward and the outward life in word, work, thoughts, and desires, to think over sin and distress freely, so that the soul may be kept in the knowledge of herself and the fear of God and may progress in there. However, this practice cannot make anyone perfect, righteous, and holy according to the law, but it is a preparation for a better hope, which better hope, better way, and better practice is that we should come to God once again like children, simply. And I do believe that it is this practice which would be much more useful and improving for you.

Could it displease God if you were to forget yourself together with all your woes, in order to remember Him and remain in Him, especially as you know that you cannot help yourself in anything, and that He alone must save? And, there would be no danger of your knowing yourself and your failings less well by deliberately examining yourself and continually gazing at your sins. You will rather realize your misery and peculiarities in a far more profitable and right way, without directly intending to do so, for you will see them in the undeceiving light of God and of His purpose. In it, sins humble, but they do not disquieten, they do not make us discouraged.

What we deny is not annihilated by our denial. The annihilation is God's business more than ours. I deny something with which I want to have nothing more to do, which I no longer want to recognize as mine, from which I withdraw my heart and consent, and which I no longer want to see. And, if we do this in respect of ourselves and of all evil, then God does the rest, and we have nothing to do but look to Him and wait for His help with patience. In this way the Lord fights for us, and we can be at peace.

Since you cannot *do* much to love and praise Him, suffer, as it is given to you from moment to moment, in love and praise to Him.

Outwardly narrow, inwardly wide, is my old rule.

Love prayer more than reading. But the child-like prayer of the heart is what I mean. Read also more with the heart than with the head, and, therefore, only such writings as can nourish and strengthen the heart.

Dear Brother,

Your note and your verses are most refreshing to me. God grant that He confirm it all with His Holy Spirit. I identify thyself heartily with your thought. God's faithfulness and our ingratitude and disloyalty are deeps. Deep calleth unto deep, as David says. We are moved, constrained, and awakened every time we think of that. O that I might, with you, be faithful to such a God of all grace as our God! I await it and beg it from His mercy for you and for myself. Only, dear brother, when we look on such deeps we must not be alarmed, but peacefully sink into them. So what must be accomplished according to God's purpose will be accomplished.

Souls, called to true spiritual life, must receive all impressions, illumination, and grace as passively as possible, leaving them just where they have been received. When such souls, in all good faith, bring what God gives to the spirit too far into the senses, the effect appears at first to increase; they become very fervent or sensitive or contented, while, all unnoticed, the spirit grows dull and dry. Something of this sort, I think, has happened to you too. Sometimes our senses are moved to devotion without any participation of the spirit. There are tears of joy, etc., and these we must not check, but everything must end in the annihilation of self-will and complete surrender to God. At the beginning, and in the case of those who have no vocation, it is otherwise. God is God, unchangeable in His love and loveliness, whether we can see or feel it or not. Let us base everything on THE FAITH, a secret and general acknowledgment or fundamental impression of God, by which the soul is moved to leave itself and all things, to cleave only to that hidden treasure so near to us in Christ.

I cannot do any more. Indeed, I did not think I could have done so much. Remember me,

Your poor brother,

Mülheim,

3rd May, 1738.

The Hermit's Cell

I John. iv. 16.

"In the world ye shall have tribulation":
Lord Jesus, Thou saidst it of old.
There dark are the desolate mountains,
The night winds are cold.

But safe from the storm and the tempest
My soul hath a cell;
There ever, beside the still waters,
With Jesus I dwell.

There, hushed from the strife and the sorrow,
Alone and apart,
In chambers of peace and of stillness—
That Home is His Heart.

7

Doubts and Introspection

Yes, you are quite right to regard that sinful part which moves against your will as something foreign and no concern of yours. This is a very important and necessary stage on the road to inward peace.

Our sins are like these poisonous evil beasts, which, if we keep on looking at them, not only strike terror into us, but become even more savage and leap upon us. It is quite enough to turn from them in displeasure and flee to God, that He may help you and hide you in His presence. Every day keep remembering God, our loving Father, who is present with us, and the remembrance of Him will keep you, so that even if you have to do much work with your hands, you will not be superficial nor given over to outward things in your heart.

If you have not a God you can perceive, have a God you can believe.

My dearest brother: You make much too much of the blasphemous, mocking thoughts and the doubts that come into your head as to the truth of holy Scripture and your own state. For God's sake despise and forget such things as are a burden to you and not a joy; it is not worthwhile even to turn and look at them. Make no attempt to defend yourself against them and do not even examine in how far this or that doubt has any foundation. By such examination you would give importance to something unimportant. Faith lies in the depths; we have it, we know it, and we have believed it for a long time now.

To give an example from politics. People know and believe in England that George is the rightful king. Nobody pays much attention if a poor highlander in Scotland has his doubts. Parliament is not summoned to investigate such doubts. Nobody gives a thought to the protests of the Pretender. If anyone did, he would only give them an importance they do not possess. The atheists in us and around us are only stiffened and strengthened when these scruples are so carefully examined and answered. Let us answer as a country lad answered his pastor when he was asked: "What do you do when you find something in the Bible you cannot understand?" "I think," said the boy, "God is wiser than I and He will understand all right." Let us try to believe what we believe without troubling with the conflicts of reason. The exile in the Scottish Highlands (to keep my metaphor) will have to listen to disloyal talk now and again. But patience! Next time we go to London, we won't need to do much asking, we will soon see with our own eyes who is king in England.

If it relieves you, I will gladly accept with patience and sympathy whole catalogues of your distresses, needs and sins. If only you could send them off and never look at them again like a letter you seal up and give to the post.

Fancies may possess your imagination, but, if only you take no pleasure in them, you need not feel uneasy about them.

Your previous letter and now this note, I read with amazement—amazement, not at your sins, distress, etc., but at the continual harping on yourself which is the greatest part of your misery. What business of yours is yourself!

If a distraction or a thought comes, you must aim at forgetting it, not by forcing yourself but by paying no attention to it. You should at once distract yourself for the sake of God in outward works. If you are still unable to free yourself, you must renew in your spirit that complete surrender to God by which you vowed to be His forever, by a gentle, but inward act of presenting your whole self to God. Aim, then, at remaining privately there. If the distractions still come in spite of that, you must still continue to sacrifice yourself quietly and wholeheartedly to God with your inner will. If it takes a long time and you cannot by any means wean yourself from them, take it as a cross from the Lord's hand and bear it to please Him.

Believe that you are full of sins but do not love the sins; do not worry yourself because of the sins, and so you will soon be holy and find rest for your soul.

There are still many more sins in you than you are aware of.

Yes, if God did not influence you by His Grace, you would do nothing but sin continually. We imagine that we do believe this; but everything goes to prove the contrary. How else comes it that we are so overwhelmed and downcast when we fail, or when the Lord lets us feel our sinfulness painfully and plainly as though we could touch it with our hands? Is it not because we did not think that we still had this or that in us, because we considered we had progressed farther than that? Or, perhaps, because we considered much to be virtuous which the Lord sets before our eyes as selfishness and impurity. All our efforts, in so far as they are ours, are impure, even when they aim at goodness. If anybody really believed that, he would certainly learn how to stand back from his actions and commit himself completely to the Lord.

Even when all the powers of sin and wickedness are active within you, and you are aware of nothing but temptations on every side, say sincerely to God: "Lord, in spite of this, I *will* not sin." Withdraw your inward will *gently* but completely from the evil and incline yourself inwardly to God as best you can. In Him and with Him no evil can reach you. If you cannot do even this, then suffer quietly, as a rock suffers the raging of the sea and a tree hailstorms and thunder, until bright weather returns.

A restless heart is already half-conquered and can never do any good. Certainly, when the wily serpent notices that you are afraid of every shadow, it will torment you properly, even if it achieves no more than waste of your soul's time by keeping it in continuous unrest.

So now my dear brother thinks he has lost his faith. No! What is it then, that makes you so discontented with your own condition? Why is everything that moves within you against God such torture to you? What is it that makes you so distressed and worried about whether your prayers are sincere, whether your actions please God, or whether you have faith? All that is nothing else but *faith*!

It is indeed pitiful enough that you are proud of yourself when some good motive stirs within you; in the meantime don't pay so much attention to these foolish ideas that you leave some good undone because of them.

Bread That Strengtheneth Man's Heart

John. vi. 35.

Man, earthy of the earth, an-hungered feeds
On earth's dark poison tree—
Wild gourds, and deadly roots, and bitter weeds;
And as his food is he.
And hungry souls there are, that find and eat
God's manna day by day—
And glad they are, their life is fresh and sweet,
For as their food are they.

8

Encouragement

God has patience with you, and I have patience with you, too; compose yourself in patience, then, and do not be so tiresome. What is it, then? Are you so upset because you are seeing yourself again? Do you not know, then, that in you dwells no good thing? If you remain in the *childlike ground*, then, in so far, you are out of yourself, and from that moment it is not your life but grace. When you say "All my Christianity is mere hypocrisy and falsehood; I try to escape suffering," you yourself are speaking; you are looking at yourself; and that is all partly true; but, according to the other part, the very ground of your personality, it is untrue; I know that part better than you, and I hope you will believe me when you cannot believe yourself.

As long as we want to be different from what God wants us to be at the time, we are only tormenting ourselves to no purpose.

Whenever you are aware of mistakes and impurity of heart, self-love, self-seeking, willfulness, desire, or the movements of certain emotions—whenever you are subject to distractions, just turn away from them every time, humbly and gently. Be sincerely confident in God and desire with your whole will-power never to be faithless again and never again to love what is impure. And even if this should occur a thousand times in one day, keep on doing the same again until you stand more firmly and sanely.

To be unwilling to sin: the intention is certainly necessary. Fear of sin is good, too. But, to will to keep oneself from sin—that is presumption.

It sounds incredible when you say in your letter you foresee that you would insult God. The poor child looks at his frail limbs and the great mountain and he feels like crying tearfully: "I can never get over it." Don't cry, child. Just give your loving father a loving word and lean on his arm, then you will go gently and easily over the mountain.

You insult God when you turn from Him, seeking loyalty in yourself where there is nothing but weakness and misery. Forget yourself: think of your business as much as is necessary, but no more than that. Do everything to the Lord, not to men. Overlook much when people behave contrary to your will.

Well! You cannot be reconciled to seeing your-self so wretched from every point of view. You would like to be perfectly holy and pure, and you can see and feel only the very opposite in yourself. Well now, just accept your wretchedness and close your eyes. God will surely make you holy, but you shall not see your holi-ness so that you will not give yourself airs.

Our miseries, however deep and unspeakably numerous, shall in no wise hinder us, but rather urge us on to sink away from ourselves and surrender ourselves to the love of God which is eternal and so inwardly near. His wise and powerful hands can build up on our nothingness a great house of holiness to His everlasting glory.

All the powers of hell cannot force you to con-sent to a single sin. As long as you remain in death, passivity, and surrender, you can walk unharmed in the midst of the flames.

If the enemy, if our corrupt part, wants to rage and roar, then the spirit takes nothing to do with him—just says "no," means it, and keeps calm.

You do not want to sin, but if it should happen, nevertheless, or, when you think it has happened, recall it and give yourself over to God afresh.

If your surrender to God is complete, then the peace or rest of the soul in God is complete, too. There are no half measures.

For timid temperaments, even when they are devoted to God, it is no uncommon temptation to allow the self to become so weak and helpless through fearful imaginings of what is to come that they often cannot cope with the present worthily because they are at grips with some problem of the future.

For many a one death seems terrifying at a distance, but desirable when it is present. Others are heroes from afar and fearful when it comes to the test.

It all depends on the grace of God; if God is there, then the tiniest, poorest child can look death in the face fearlessly.

His goodness can far more easily evaporate your misery than red-hot iron a raindrop.

"The Sun to Rule by Day"

Phil. ii. 13.

Thou sayest, "Fit me, fashion me for Thee."
Stretch forth thine empty hands, and be thou still;
O restless soul, thou dost but hinder Me
By valiant purpose and by steadfast will.
Behold the summer flowers beneath the sun,
In stillness his great glory they behold;
And sweetly thus his mighty work is done,
And resting in his gladness they unfold.
So are the sweetness and the joy divine
Thine, O belovèd, and the work is Mine.

9

Sincerity, True and False

An apparent reason and expedient which erring souls produce as a cloak for their free and easy way of life is: "I cannot be a hypocrite. I must show myself outwardly as I am inwardly." So, if they are inwardly disposed or naturally biased to pride and evil, they feel unable and unwilling to appear better than they really are.

Well, it is certainly true that God abhors nothing so much as lies, cunning pretences, and hypocrisy, and that nothing therefore hinders us so much on our way to union with Him as our hidden insincerity; yes, that far more than our sinfulness itself! But we all start life so permeated with this pernicious leaven, that it takes years for even the most sincere characters to become thoroughly cleansed and healed from it.

For true sincerity, it is not required that when we do or show forth good we should feel in ourselves no reluctance or impulses to evil; but it is necessary to do everything that we do outwardly with the single aim to please not men but God, because we want to be in our hearts inwardly what we act outwardly—e.g., I am naturally inclined to love jokes and smart clothes, so I must avoid entirely all frivolity in clothes and words. Indeed, at the beginning, and as long as this inclination is still strong and fundamental to my personality, I must compel myself forcibly—not in the least to make plain to myself or others that I am now a humbler and more serious man, for this would be self-deception and hypocrisy, but, firstly, that I will not nourish and strengthen inner corruption with outward actions; and, secondly, to show God and man, by this self-denial, that in spite of all impulses to the contrary of which, to my sorrow I am conscious, I have now received from God a new mind and will which is the enemy of evil. And I would not be a hypocrite, I would be sincere because I would now show outwardly what I love and desire inwardly. It would be deception of the worst kind if I went about it otherwise and denied by my evil actions my private good intentions.

In your first resolve to serve God, you give Him your will and your assent, imperfect though it be, as it were in its tender seed. From that moment, then, this intention lies planted in the soul. "Yes, Lord, this evil is no use. O that I were free from it! Yes, Lord! I must become holy. O, if only I could put it into practice!"

If such a man, in whose heart is such a purpose to goodness, resists evil by the grace of God and holds it back so that it does not break forth, he is not being a hypocrite, he is going to work sincerely. However many evil impulses rise within him against his will to goodness, he will deny them; that is to say, he will not recognize them as his. He won't hold with them; he won't give his consent and will not follow them. If any-one does not resist evil as much as he can in this way, either his mind has not been moved and he is there-fore an unrepentant child of this world, or he is not going about it sincerely, holding inwardly to God and blessedness, but behaving outwardly as if he held with the world and vanity.

The High Calling

Ps. xlv. 9.

Child of the Eternal Father,
Bride of the Eternal Son,
Dwelling-place of God the Spirit,
Thus with Christ made ever one;
Dowered with joy beyond the Angels
Nearest to His throne,
They, the ministers attending
His beloved one:
Granted all my heart's desire,
All things made my own;
Feared by all the powers of evil,
Fearing God alone;
Walking with the Lord in glory
Through the courts divine,
Queen within the royal palace,
Christ for ever mine;
Say, poor worldling, can it be,
That my heart should envy thee?

10

True Religion

Everything, however plausible, which withdraws us from love and brings us into unrest, must be suspect.

Nature is so fond of bogs that weak characters lose themselves happily in them, but never reach the sea because they have no *fall.* That is why I talk little, and then only in private, about ways (guidance) because of the pride which so wants to read before it has learned to spell. Very few attain grace of humility in their own souls. Some want to bypass it, others have no fall or else they do not give themselves up to it from moment to moment with complete surrender.

We, too, know that outward things and outward means are only forms, and not the spirit itself. But who knows whether those who want to have it all at once without forms, are not playing with other forms which have still less of the spirit? God himself took form to make us spiritual: yes, He became a child to put us mighty ones down from our seats.[6]

But you must know that it is not love when you feel the loveliness of God, or when everything in Christianity seems so easy and jolly. This is good, and it is a gift of God; but love of God is really wanting with all one's heart to please God to the best of one's ability.

[6] *Magnificat:* "He hath put down the mighty from their seat."

ACTIVITY, WISE AND FOOLISH

A certain amount of movement and external affairs are good from time to time. It is not work which brings harm so long as the work goes no farther than your hands and the outer man; but your heart stays with God.

Let our real work be apart from us and everything. All else, even the edification of our neighbor, must only be in passing and with great moderation.

Although I do say that you must behave passively toward the working of God, I do not on that account condemn all activity. You must be active when God makes you active; only, let everything be done gently, calmly and without strain.

It is not in the least necessary for you to probe so carefully in retrospect to find out if your will did not waver somehow. Acknowledge your failings in it all. Apart from this, see to it that you leave off thinking of evil—and the sooner the better—and sink yourself more and more in the God who loves you. Not evil, not what you have done, not this, nor that, but God alone, must be your preoccupation.

My warm regards to your wife; she has an anxious temperament and must therefore see to it all her anxiety is directed to this one end, how she may best please the Lord in everything. Oh, that this might be her work, her most important work, her favorite work from morning till evening!

Listen, soul! Just let all your twisting and turning stop. The more you want to improve matters, the more you spoil them; the more you want to act yourself to do some good, the more mistakes you make. Working on your own is no use whatever.

Suffering for God's sake is better than working miracles.

Within Him, All Things

Is. xii. 2.

Hath not each heart a passion and a dream?
Each some companionship for ever sweet?
And each in saddest skies some silver gleam,
And each some passing joy, too fair and fleet?
And each a staff and stay, though frail it prove,
And each a face he fain would ever see?
And what have I? An endless Heaven of love,
A rapture, and a glory, and a calm;
A life that is an everlasting Psalm,
All, O Beloved, in Thee.

11

Living with Our Fellow Men

Where two people live together, a slight mistake does as much harm as a sin elsewhere; because we endanger not only our own soul, but by infection and bad example we endanger our companion's. Keep near to the Lord, so that, just as He is a light, you may both become a light in Him to the blessing of many.

Forced friendliness, helpfulness, and other evidences of love by words, looks, or deeds achieve nothing. If you each let yourself be grounded in true humility, then this external behavior flows out of itself. But, if you try to appear very friendly without having this grounding, it does no good, but sometimes even harm.

Take care only to say the bare essentials about outward things, let people think what they will.

Careless speech and thought often bring forth evil speech and thought.

I love all awakened souls; but I cannot help it that the outflow of my love is less forced to some than to others. To some, one goes out in love, but others one finds in it (in our source), and they bring no hindrance to our fellowship with God. O, how good are such friends who do not want to take us away from the Best of Friends who wants to be all and in all to us!

If the topic is outward trivial things, this or that opinion or speculation in spiritual matters which do not concern the fundamentals of salvation, we must avoid all quarreling about it and treat the matter as a temptation of the devil. But if we are desired to give our opinion and knowledge about this or that, then sincerity demands that, if it is considered edifying, we should state it as we know it, although others may have other opinions. But it must be done without presumption, heat, or stubbornness. And so it is neither necessary nor edifying to attack sharply others who talk about something which does not agree with what we know about it, and who stick stubbornly to their opinion when we think the contrary. Of course, we must not accept something as good and true when inwardly we have other light on it; but, because we are men who are liable to errors in thinking, and because our knowledge in spiritual matters is fragmentary, we must not contradict violently or at great length, but, in all friendliness we must leave such a one to his own thoughts and admit that we too may be wrong. Indeed, we thought otherwise in the past and had other ideas than we now have—and who knows where we will stand in the future?

Take care, in so far as God gives you grace, that this right and proper sympathy which you both have for them in their present circumstances, does not penetrate too far into your hearts, so that by it you are swayed and made restless, depressed, and darkened and even your body becomes weak and still less service-able.

Do not look at things in a human way, but in God and His will, who rules all things and turns to the good of His poor creatures what they by their own fault have spoiled.

And so you will understand, dear brother, that I am not advising you against all intercourse with friends or with books. I am only warning you against excess, and against wanting to know everything without examining or discriminating before passing judgment and permitting oneself the ideas on the friendship. The test is quite simple. Whatever strengthens us in the main thing, whatever enters into our spirit without force, and whatever calms us during our time of meditation and prayer, is good for us. The rest is not.

If I were your confessor or director, I would impose on you as a wholesome penance every time you sinned by giving way to these tempers, to confess at once frankly to those present, even if only to a servant, a child, or a man. And this seems to me useful for several reasons.

As to social intercourse, my advice is still friendship with all good people, but intimacy with few. And if divine providence gives us so very few whom we try

and find worthy, then let these few be the more precious and the more dear to us the rarer they are these
days—provided we don't make idols of them.

When you notice lack of affection, or some
other ill-feeling in others toward you, think no evil.
Believe that they do not mean wickedness, but the devil
is present there, trying to rouse your temper, unsettle
you and involve you. Pluck the evil eye out of yourself
at once, by abruptly but gently turning away your feel-
ings and your thoughts from other people to your own
inward poverty, or to the presence of God in your own
heart.

Giving-in is a truly God-like virtue, and you can
work miracles with it. And you can seldom go too far in

it: for there is only one thing to which we must never give in, and that is the will to sin.

Greeting people is an inward bowing of our good-will and love; it is the invisible handshake of the spirit, by which we really give each other as much as we have of God's grace, strength, peace, and life.

The Summer Day

Can. i. 7.

. . . .

Alone with Thee to dwell, O my Beloved,
Is heaven on earth begun;
Whilst vanity of vanities outwearies
All hearts beneath the Sun.
Alone with Thee to dwell, O my Beloved,
Is heaven on earth begun;
Above the midnight and the noonday glory,
Our resting-place is won.
Alone with Thee to dwell, O my Beloved,
Is heaven on earth begun;
And Thou my joy, mine everlasting Heaven,
My pilgrim journey done.

12

Marriage

I give you for your consideration the words from St. John's gospel, chapter 2: "Both Jesus was called, and His disciples, to the marriage." This must also be said of your wedding, so that, later, when your water-pots are filled with the waters of affliction, for marriage is a state wedded to affliction, the Lord Jesus may change it into the pure wine of spiritual blessing and comfort. And this I desire for you with all my heart.

I know various religious married couples who are very intimate in the natural life, but complete strangers to each other in the spiritual life. This is no use, and it is a bad sign. Let each tell the other his good and his bad simply like a child. Carry one another, remind one another, pray with one another, love one another, and begin your life together as you wish it may end. God grant that the world may see in you proof that there can be true saints in the married state also.

The Quiet Land

Deut. xxvi. 9.

Stillness midst the ever-changing,
Lord, my rest art Thou;
So for me has dawned the morning,
God's eternal NOW.
Now for me the day unsetting,
Now the song begun;
Now, the deep surpassing glory,
Brighter than the sun.
Hail! all hail! thou peaceful country
Of eternal calm;
Summer land of milk and honey,
Where the streams are balm.
There the Lord my Shepherd leads me,
Wheresoe'er He will;
In the fresh green pastures feeds me,
By the waters still.
Well I know them, those still waters!
Peace and rest at last;
In their depths the quiet heavens
Tell the storms are past,
Nought to mar the picture fair,
Of the glory resting there.

13

Serenity

Make room for everything which is capable of rejoicing, enlarging or calming your heart, in a child-like spirit; but seek nothing restlessly. What is taken from you, just let go. God Himself you will keep for ever; or rather He will keep you.

Nothing is more beautiful than simply to make room for God—without an act of will, without using the imagination and without the aid of forms. In outward and inward detachment from such things, let yourself be permeated by God and His love.

May God fulfill in you also His precious promise, and lure you more and more out of yourself and all created things! May He lead you into the sweet wilderness of inner solitude, and there speak to your soul like a friend. God's speaking is creative. He creates peace, innocence, simplicity, kindness, love, humility, and all the virtues in our hearts.

Avoid all violent outbursts of emotion. The best and holiest desires must end in the peaceful inward calm of God. It must not be so much a breathing-out as a breathing-in, or a gentle inclining to the Lord in your heart.

When we are quiet children of suffering, and extinguish all the power of anger in ourselves and in others with pure love, then Jesus comes in and sups with us.

May the Lord bring all that is ours to a profound silence!

Within the Holiest

Rev. i. 5, 6.

His priest am I, before Him day and night,
Within His Holy Place;
And death, and life, and all things dark and bright,
I spread before His Face.
Rejoicing with His joy, yet ever still,
For silence is my song;
My work to bend beneath His blessed will,
All day, and all night long—
For ever holding with Him converse sweet,
Yet speechless, for my gladness is complete.

14

The Inner Life

He well understands how to discover in our heart that innermost nook of sincerity which tends toward Him. There He can live; yes, there He can really live even when everything else in us is taken up by a thousand temptations and all sorts of involuntary wickedness. There we must aim to live and hide ourselves again and again, in there with Him, in all simplicity and quietness.

The urge to the inner life is an urge to be hid with Him.

The inner life is much less known than one would imagine, even among those who have been called.

To pick up a straw with loving intention is more to God than to remove mountains without love.

Dear Child,

You do well to write now and then and tell me how things are with you; but always do so in a childlike spirit, as it comes, without wondering if you are doing the right thing, and how I will take it. And you must accept my answer in the same childlike spirit, whether I reply only in the spirit, or with the pen as well. Believe this one thing steadfastly, that I love your soul sincerely, and am inexpressibly glad when you try to live with God in childlike faith and childlike love.

Whatever your state may be, never let anyone rob you of these two fundamental truths: (1) that God *is present* everywhere, and particularly in your heart; (2) that God loves you dearly and would have you entirely for Himself.

The air in which we live is near us; the air is in us and we are in the air. God is infinitely nearer; we live and move in God; we eat, drink, and work in God; we think in God, and (don't be startled because I put it like this) anyone who commits a sin, sins in God. This presence of God is incomprehensible; we cannot and we must not picture it, but believe simply that it is so.

How then, dear heart, can outward unrest, business or people distract you from God, as you complain, since you are living in God all the time and everything exists and everything happens in God? Should we forget the sunlight in which we live? Should we not remember our God, worship Him, love Him, and praise Him in the midst of all our affairs and relationships which, in God's presence, are smaller than a speck of dust in the sunlight?

Accept everything then (with the sole exception of sin) as from the hand of God; do all your work as in God's sight and in God, in as simple and childlike a spirit as you can. And just as we are glad when the sun shines, so that we can do our work, be glad inwardly that you have God as a close friend in whom everywhere and at all times, outwardly and inwardly, you can work, live, move, die, and love. Now God is, as I have just said, really present everywhere; but, because He is a spirit, He is present in quite a special and more blessed way to our spirit. God is more inward than our most intimate thought. There He calls us, there He waits for us. He wants to impart Himself to us and make us blessed. This presence, too, we must believe in simply, without understanding it, yes, even without wanting to be always conscious of it.

And so, our spirit within us is God's workshop, temple, and shrine, where God lives and desires to live; and, as often as we turn there like children, sincerely, with our love, our longing, and our heart's devotion, and keep ourselves in this faith in His presence, we go to our church and take part in a solemn service. If we are not yet as blessed as they that dwell in God's House, ever praising Him (as Psalm 84 has it) we should always desire this, and with our desires and loving thoughts always be there, even in our business; just as the Jews always had to turn their faces toward the temple wherever in the world they might be.

I will put it more simply. It is as if there were a little secret room in your heart where your best friend lives and waits for you. And so your love must urge you now and again to purchase some time, and if possible some outward loneliness, so that you can go to your friend in the little room and talk to him privately, and tell him how you are and that you want to love him truly. And when you go back again to your business, let it be as if you took your friend by the hand and begged him to come with you and keep you company while you work, and take care of you. And that he will do most willingly.

And when, during your work you turn your thoughts and your love to Him, just as a child would, and ask if you can do everything *for Him*, then it cannot possibly go ill with you in any kind of business or among any sort of people.

Don't worry if you cannot understand everything I write. You don't need it all: take a little crumb from the dish for yourself and let N. and N. take some too.

Remember Jesus and forget yourself.

Mülhiem,
29th February, 1736.

The Habitation of God

Ps. xxvii. 4.

Here on earth a temple stands,
Temple never built with hands;
There the Lord doth fill the place
With the glory of His grace.
Cleansed by Christ's atoning Blood,
Thou art this fair House of God.
Thoughts, desires, that enter there,
Should they not be pure and fair?
Meet for holy courts and blest,
Courts of stillness and of rest,
Where the soul, a priest in white,
Singeth praises day and night;
Glory of the love divine
Filling all this heart of thine.

15

One Holy Church

I believe that in the eyes of God there are really only two sets of people on earth: the children of the world in whom love of the world rules, and the children of God into whom the love of God is poured by His Holy Spirit; and that, apart from this, God pays no attention to any difference or name.

To live *wholly for God* is the true secret of that inner or mystic life of which people make such strange and terrible pictures. There is nothing simpler, surer, lovelier, and more fruitful than this life of the heart, which we can know and experience completely not by reading or racking the brains, but by dying and loving.

The true inner life is no strange or new thing; it is the ancient and true worship of God, the Christian life in its beauty and in its own peculiar form. Truly inward souls make no particular sects; if each one followed the teaching and life of Jesus by His Spirit, then, without any doubt, everyone would live the inner life and the world would be full of mystics.

Some let themselves be led astray by the cunning serpent, astray from simplicity into the harmful heights of reason, and waste their precious time in useless speculations and the investigation of all sorts of secrets of nature; they want to set themselves to seek the philosopher's stone and the key of the universe. This is the golden apple which has hindered many a good soul of our time in his race, and made him fall into the deepest misery of soul and body.

Whether he knows what I think of separation, Church government, or, as he calls it, sectarianism, or whether he doesn't, can help neither his soul nor mine. And whether our opinions on that subject are similar or different does not make us one hair's breadth the holier or more blessed.

When I have the chance of hearing a godly Reformed or Lutheran preacher, I go to church; and if I had the chance of getting to know a godly Catholic preacher, I would listen to his sermon in the very same freedom of spirit; although I might not always avail myself of this freedom because of the weaknesses of others.

Wherever there is a man who fears God and lives the good life, in any country under the sun, God is there, loving him, and so I love him too, whatever religious coat he may be wearing; and so, it is quite true, I do go about with people of all sorts of religious persuasions. I talk to them publicly or privately, as God disposes, about denying God, about prayer and about loving God and I let the whole edifice of their particular Church government and doctrine stand quite untouched, as long as God lets it stand.

I waste little or no time on particular doctrines, not even on the popular official doctrines of many denominations—the fall of antichrist, the millennium, purification, the Second Coming, and such like.

Dying to myself and to all creation that I may live God in Jesus Christ, is the whole secret of my faith.

That such shining examples of holy souls are little known among the Protestants has many causes. The freedom we have to believe, read, speak, and do as we please, is often misused in many and various distractions and hindrances. We are *spectators* not *actors*—onlookers, not doers.

I believe what the saints say; but only because they say it, without going deeply into their particular opinions which leave no trace of influence on me. But anything which touches or aims at the center of the inner life I cling to, and I find myself in intimate union with them there.

Love alone is not walled in by divisions, love is universal; it flows out into the infinite, for it proceeds from the Father and the Son and takes into its wide embrace all who will let themselves be gathered in. And it is my hope that soon all the scattered children of God will creep in once more to this, the true fold of the Church, and, without any of the labors, forms, and contrivings of man, become one blessed flock with one Shepherd. For love will win in the end, but it will be that pure love of God which is poured out in true fellowship with the Father and the Son in the hearts of those who strive to walk in the light, turning from the shadow to the substance, from the outer to the inner, and from all multiplicity to the one thing needful. This alone brings us union with one another and peace with God.

At Rest

Is. xl. 11.

O God, a world of empty show,
Dark wilds of restless, fruitless quest
Lie round me wheresoe'er I go:
Within, with Thee, is rest.

And sated with the weary sum
Of all men think, and hear, and see,
O more than mother's heart, I come,
A tired child to Thee.

Sweet childhood of eternal life!
Whilst troubled days and years go by,
In stillness hushed from stir and strife,
Within Thine Arms I lie.

Thine Arms, to whom I turn and cling
With thirsting soul that longs for Thee;
As rain that makes the pastures sing,
Art Thou, my God, to me.

16

War and Peace[7]

We see and hear, alas, amid all the misery in the world, much indignation and lamentation over the nations at war, but little repentance and lamentation for sin and forgetfulness of God.

God wants to waken us from our sleep by the noise and pressure. He does not want the dogs He has sent to disperse the sheep, but to gather them together and drive them to Himself. He takes our idols away from us; He makes it hard for us in the world so that we can let ourselves go completely and turn from it all, inwards to Him and dear, blessed eternal life; also, that we should make haste to be made perfect.

[7] Written during the Seven Years' War.

may He soon command the sword to be sheathed and the tumult to cease; meanwhile, may He give us and preserve to us His precious peace of heart which the world cannot give, and which no enemy can take away, because it is too deep and is rooted in God.

Meanwhile, whether peace be or war, the evening of our life comes hastening on and our work lies unfinished.

Evensong

Ps. xci. 4.

Take me, Jesus, to Thy breast;
Folded close in warmth and rest,
Keep me near to Thee;
Silenced in the bliss profound
Of the love that wraps me round,
Every care shall be.
Every breath for Thee alone,
O my heart's beloved One;
Comfort me in sleep.
Still deep rest art Thou to Thine,
Safely in Thine arms divine
Thy beloved keep.

17

Tersteegen's Portrait in His Letters

And if I were a saint, I could do no better service than to turn you away from me and from all creation toward Him, who is Himself life.

I have been away from home twice for the sake of two sorely-tried souls. On Friday I came back from S—— P.F. took me there by post-chaise, and he, with the other awakened souls, was most unwilling to let me go. So I must give myself up and go blindfolded how and where the Master wills.

Never accept from me or any other creature anything which does not lead you to God and calm and broaden, not your sensual nature, but your center and soul.

Since I know that there is little or nothing in me which could be helpful to others, I have to tell the

Lord not to leave souls who, because of His grace, have confidence in me.

We who utter the Word are like organ pipes, giving the tune, but here and there in a cottage sits a simple, inward soul who, by his secret prayers fills us with the breath of the Spirit with its power and blessing both for ourselves and for others.

My bodily weakness comes and goes. Head and eyes are very weak, and at times I cannot write anything. But may the Lord let no leaf, however tiny, fall to the ground from the rood-tree and die!

Indeed, for a few days, it seemed as if I were recovering; but my health, I can feel, is unreliable. If only the scaffolding stands till the building is complete, then the short and easy sufferings will soon fly past.

You write to brother H. that you do not know where I am. But now you will easily be able to see that by

God's providence I am still on my journey to the quiet of eternity, where I hope to arrive in due time.

Oh, what living and painful proof it is of the rarity of enlightenment in these days, and the spiritual privation among the elect, when I see them revere such a slight measure of grace in me (although it is far more than I deserve) and look up to me, who, in my estimation, could scarcely be missed on earth!

I would like to beg you, if I may, not to use the word "director" in letters. You yourself can think what you like. I have my reasons.

I postponed for a time my answer to my dear brother's enjoyable letter of 21st March because I am chary, and not without cause, of giving myself too much correspondence when I am otherwise so occupied and, besides, I am learning more and more. that the true Christian life to which I find myself called by the mercy of God, demands a disciplined companionship and an inner life with Him; in this way we can more nearly attain in this mortal life to the goal of our calling, namely, essential fellowship and union with God.

Our Jesus was silent for thirty years so that He might imbue us with the love of the life of withdrawal. In public life He spent scarcely four years. Often I think to myself: Oh, if we awakened souls could only endure four apprentice years of quiet praying and dying to self-will before we launched forth, then our subsequent activities would be a little purer and less injurious to the Kingdom of God in us and around us! This is the secret; but the Enemy, using the common and subtle temptations of nature, would entice us away from the ONE THING NEEDFUL and weaken our strength in a multiplicity of works. But Nature and those who follow her, for whom this life of dying becomes too narrow and vexatious, can draw breath, preserve, and strengthen themselves better by all seemingly spiritual outward activities.

And so, my precious friend, let us, to the love and glory of God, close the eyes of our spirits to all sidetracks and distractions, that we may realize in gentleness and quietness of soul nothing but our holy calling which, by His grace, once intimated itself to us and will call again in our hearts.

As for myself, I have been troubled twice again since your visit with strange attacks of weakness that I thought my "cottage" would collapse. When your last letter arrived, I was very weak; as my condition had improved somewhat, I wanted to walk for a little in the sun, but I was overcome with such faintness that I thought I would die before I reached home; palpitations, numbness, and fever followed. But God, who is merciful, has allowed me time for sanctification and set me up again, so much so that I can visit other people and help them in their frailty. My head is very weak and my body weary; but I must not think much about that; there are various people here, much more ill than I, who think my visits useful or stimulating, and therefore I am not free to keep away from them.

Dear children, do pray to God for me, that the Lord may prepare me and make the short remainder of my days fruitful to His glory!

Biographical Notes

GERHARD TERSTEEGEN was born in Moers, Germany in 1697. Abandoned by his father in early childhood, Tersteegen was thereafter raised by his mother in poverty. Wanting to study theology, but not possessing the means to afford the tuition, Tersteegen was forced to enter commerce and practiced as a successful merchant until a formative meeting with Wilhelm Hoffmann (1685-1746), a pietist revivalist, decisively changed the spiritual course of his life. Thereafter Tersteegen preferred the solitary life and gave up his merchant activities to work as a humble weaver, knitting ribbons, studying at home in cloister-like asceticism, and reading theological books. In 1728 he became an itinerant preacher in the Protestant *Erweckungsbewegung* ("Spiritual Awakening Movement") in the Niederrhein region, and hosted home worship and prayer meetings. He soon became acknowledged as an authoritative lay theologian, pastor, and mystic of the Protestant pietism movement, and was widely revered for his saintly character. Beginning in 1729, he edited his famous work, *Geistliches Blumengärtlein inniger Seelen* ("Spiritual Flower Garden for Ardent Souls"), a collection of hymns, spiritual lyrics, and epigrams. Gerhard Tersteegen died at Mülheim, in Westphalia, Germany, in 1769.

PETER C. ERB is a professor in the Religion & Culture department at Wilfrid Laurier University in Waterloo, Canada. He received his B.A. from Wilfrid Laurier, his M.S.L. from the Pontifical Institute of Medieval Studies, Toronto University, and his Ph.D. from Toronto University. His scholarly interests include the following: Roman Catholic and Protestant writers of the Romantic period; nineteenth century British theology; nineteenth century British religious novels; German Pietism; the Radical Reformation; and late medieval spirituality. Among his numerous publications are the titles *Pietists: Selected Writings*; *Pietists, Protestants, and Mysticism: The Use of Late Medieval Spiritual Texts in the Work of Gottfried Arnold (1666-1714)*; *A Question of Sovereignty: The Politics of Manning's Conversion*; and *Newman and the Idea of a Catholic University.*

Index

Index

Index of Hymns

Titles in the Spiritual Classics Series by World Wisdom

The Buddha Eye: An Anthology of the Kyoto School and Its Contemporaries, edited by Frederick Franck, 2004

A Christian Woman's Secret: A Modern-Day Journey to God, by Lilian Staveley, 2008

The Essential Writings of Charles Eastman (Ohiyesa): Light on the Indian World, edited by Michael Oren Fitzgerald, 2002

Gospel of the Redman, compiled by Ernest Thompson Seton and Julia M. Seton, 2005

An Introduction to Sufi Doctrine, by Titus Burckhardt, 2008

Lamp of Non-Dual Knowledge & Cream of Liberation: Two Jewels of Indian Wisdom, by Sri Swami Karapatra and Swami Tandavaraya, translated by Swami Sri Ramanananda Saraswathi, 2003

Music of the Sky: An Anthology of Spiritual Poetry, edited by Patrick Laude and Barry McDonald, 2004

The Mystics of Islam, by Reynold A. Nicholson, 2002

Naturalness: A Classic of Shin Buddhism, by Kenryo Kanamatsu, 2002

The Path of Muhammad: A Book on Islamic Morals and Ethics, by Imam Birgivi, interpreted by Shaykh Tosun Bayrak, 2005

Pray Without Ceasing: The Way of the Invocation in World Religions, edited by Patrick Laude, 2006

The Quiet Way: A Christian Path to Inner Peace, by Gerhard Tersteegen, translated by Emily Chisholm, 2008

Tripura Rahasya: The Secret of the Supreme Goddess, translated by Swami Sri Ramanananda Saraswathi, 2002

Titles on Christianity
by World Wisdom

*A Christian Pilgrim in India: The Spiritual Journey of
Swami Abhishiktananda (Henri Le Saux)*, by Harry Oldmeadow, 2008

A Christian Woman's Secret: A Modern-Day Journey to God,
by Lilian Staveley, 2008

Christian Spirit, edited by Judith Fitzgerald and
Michael Oren Fitzgerald, 2004

The Destruction of the Christian Tradition: Updated and Revised,
by Rama P. Coomaraswamy, 2006

For God's Greater Glory: Gems of Jesuit Spirituality,
edited by Jean-Pierre Lafouge, 2006

The Foundations of Christian Art: Illustrated,
by Titus Burckhardt, edited by Michael Oren Fitzgerald, 2006

The Fullness of God: Frithjof Schuon on Christianity,
selected and edited by James S. Cutsinger, 2004

In the Heart of the Desert: The Spirituality of the Desert Fathers and Mothers,
by John Chryssavgis, 2003

Not of This World: A Treasury of Christian Mysticism,
compiled and edited by James S. Cutsinger, 2003

Paths to the Heart: Sufism and the Christian East,
edited by James S. Cutsinger, 2002

Paths to Transcendence: According to Shankara, Ibn Arabi, and Meister Eckhart,
by Reza Shah-Kazemi, 2006

The Sermon of All Creation: Christians on Nature,
edited by Judith Fitzgerald and Michael Oren Fitzgerald, 2005

Ye Shall Know the Truth: Christianity and the Perennial Philosophy,
edited by Mateus Soares de Azevedo, 2005